THE MONKEY'S PAW

What is the price of greed? What is the cost of desire?
The White family have come to possess a relic of supernatural power, a monkey's paw that grants three wishes....but at what price? How far must they journey down the path of terror to undo what they have done? Based on the short horror tale by W.W Jacobs, "The Monkey's Paw" is a story that will have you sitting on the very edge of your seat.

THIS RESOURCE INCLUDES:

The full short screenplay for "The Monkey's Paw", the gothic horror masterpiece that can be performed and filmed in the classroom.

The comic or graphic novel of "The Monkey's Paw". A great way to visually engage with the story.

The full short stage play for "The Monkey's Paw", which can be performed in the classroom and on the stage.

Teachers notes and lesson ideas.

CHALKBOARD
THESPIANS

A Chalkboard Thespians book
www.chalkboardthespians.com

"Dramatic playing is essential for children's learning empathy and self-control. Children learn to empathize as they view the world from other people's perspectives including those of peers, adults, and people in stories."

- Brian Edmiston -

Chalkboard Thespians
www.chalkboardthespians.com

First published by Chalkboard Thespians, 2015

Copyright © 2015

Sourced through the Guggenheim Project 2014

All rights reserved. Without limiting the rights under copyright reserved above, no part of this publication may be reproduced, stored in or introduced into a retrieval system, or transmitted, in any form or by any means (electronic, mechanical, photocopying, recording or otherwise), without the prior written permission of both the copyright owner and the above publisher of this book.

Typeset in Abel and Ubuntu by April Sadowski

ISBN- 10: 1632270404
ISBN- 13: 978-1-63227-040-5

CONTENTS

Introduction

Short Screenplay "The Monkey's Paw"................. 9
(including: How to Read a Screenplay)

Comic (graphic novel) "The Monkey's Paw" 43
(including How to Read a Comic Strip)

Short Stage Play "The Monkey's Paw" 73
(including How to Read a Stage Play)

The Monkey's Paw in the classroom 109

FOREWORD: ABOUT THIS BOOK

The old educational world of texts is evolving in an incredibly exciting way as our paths to meaning expand and develop with technology. This is a book about embracing this exciting development in the classroom and marrying the ancient art of performance with a brave new world of technology and exploration. Film and theatre are all about discovering new frontiers, being bold and brave enough to challenge boundaries and above all, growing.

You will find two scripts, a stage play and a short film, and a graphic novel in this book. They are all adaptations of a Gothic Horror story by W.W Jacobs, "The Monkey's Paw", which is as disturbing today as it was over a hundred years ago when it was first written. A class can choose to study this text as a stage play to be performed in the classroom or theatre, or as a screenplay, to be performed, filmed, edited and screened or as a visual medium; exploring the world of visual literacy through the comic strip. Indeed, a class may choose to study all three and compare and contrast the disciplines, the differences and limitations that set them apart.

The scripts, although similar, are different. The original story narrative exists in the landscape of the mind, we not only hear and see the characters, but are also exposed to their thoughts and feelings on the page. The stage play exists in the landscape of the spoken word, as information is relayed only by what actors say and do, information about feelings and thoughts must be communicated in a visual and audible way. In contrast, a screenplay exists in the landscape of the visual. Information about thoughts and feelings must be communicated by what we see on the screen. Sound and music are of course a part of this also, but information is relayed in new ways, given the endless opportunities to layer images and sound.

This is a book for English, Drama and Media teachers alike, and at a rudimentary level contains scripts that can be read aloud in the classroom. The subject matter is dark, intriguing and at the least, engaging. But beyond this it is also an entry point into short film, which can be studied through the website **www.chalkboardthespians.com**, and will take a class from concept to screen with little to no budget. Above all, it is a book of initiative and innovation, opening the door to possibilities and hopefully empowering a new generation of teachers and students to express themselves and make meaning.

ABOUT THE AUTHOR:

Shane Emmett is an actor, international award-winning filmmaker and high school teacher. Completing a degree in Media and Communications in Sydney in 1998, he began his career working as a professional actor in Musical theatre, performing roles ranging from Marius in "Les Miserables", to Frank Marlow in "Get Happy". In 2003 he wrote, produced and performed the musical "From Here to Eternity" the Frank Sinatra story.

Shane continues to work as a television actor, playing "Mark Gilmour" on Home and Away throughout 2011, and also playing regular roles on series such as All Saints, Offspring, Rush, Power Games and Precinct 13.

He also continues to work as a filmmaker, writing and producing a number of international award-winning short films. His short film "Mankind is no Island" was shot on a mobile phone and won Best Film at Tropfest New York. It was later awarded the Inside Film (IF) award for Best Short Documentary in 2009.

Above all he has also worked as an English high school teacher in Australia for seventeen years and continues to be a champion of drama and film in the classroom.

HOW TO READ A SCREENPLAY

Just like a movie, a screenplay is divided into scenes. These are numbered on the left hand side of the page. Each scene has a heading that starts with INT or EXT. This tells you if the scene is interior (inside) or exterior (outside). This is followed by the location of the scene and the time of day.

e.g.   **INT. INDUSTRIAL FACTORY. DAY**

Underneath the heading is a description of what we see in the scene and the general direction. This is always written in present tense and is sometimes referred to as "the business". When there is a centred character's name in capital letters, it is followed by dialogue by that character.

                          MR WHITE
e.g.:   Listen to the wind!

If there are words in brackets in the dialogue, this is a direction for the character's performance. Sometimes there might be directions for the camera shots also in the script that use abbreviations such as **CU** (close up), **LS** (long shot), **MS** (mid-shot).

At the right of the page are editing transitions to move from scene to scene. This will either be a straight cut from one scene to the other **CUT TO:**, but can sometimes fade one scene into the other **FADE TO:** or fade to black **FADE TO BLACK**.

Sometimes we only hear the voice of a character but visually see something else. This is indicated with **VO** (voice over). Finally when a character is talking and is interrupted with an action or direction in the script, their dialogue indicates that it continues with a **(CONT'D)**.

Above all, try to read the screenplay like a movie would play out. It is often good to get one person to read the scene headings and business and get actors to read the dialogue for each character.

THE MONKEY'S PAW

SCREENPLAY

ADAPTED BY
SHANE EMMETT

BASED ON THE STORY BY W.W. JACOBS

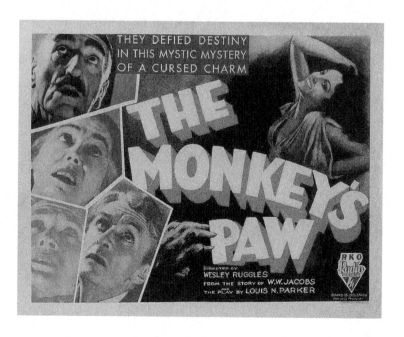

Character Breakdown

Mr. White: Patriarch of the White family. He is an older man who cares deeply for his wife and son. He is retired from working at the local Maw and Meggins factory.

Mrs White: Matriarch of the White family. She is an older woman who cares deeply for her husband and son.

Major Morris: A Sergeant Major with a distinguished military record. He worked with Mr White at the factory as a younger man and is a friend of the family.

Herbert White: The adult son of Mr and Mrs White. He is a happy-go-lucky man who sees humour in many situations. He works at the Maw and Meggins factory.

Gentleman: A representative from the local factory, Maw and Meggins.

Screenplay

INT. INDUSTRIAL FACTORY. DAY

Black screen. We hear an explosion of shattering glass, voices shouting in warning, a shrill scream, followed by more urgent shouts and a growing murmur of noise.

                                      FADE IN:

Factory workers all crowd around, obscuring the view. The vision fades in and out of focus, beating like a heart. A few men try and hold the growing crowd back with shouts. One gentleman we follow in a workers cap and moustache stretches above the crowd craning for a look. He pales and swoons as the horror is revealed to him, he turns and throws up.

                                      FADE TO
                                      BLACK.

EXT. LABURNAM VILLA. NIGHT

A small cottage is dimly lit at the end of a barren stretch of muddy road. Rain pounds relentlessly. The scene is cold, drab and eerie.

INT. SMALL COTTAGE PARLOUR. NIGHT

Inside Laburnam Villa, a fire crackles in a modest hearth offering little light and warmth in the small parlour. Through the drawn blinds we see the rain beating down amidst the howling wind. An old man, Mr. White sits opposite his son, Herbert White passing the time playing chess on a rustic table. Closer to the fire sits Mrs White, a white haired old lady knitting placidly.

The Monkey's Paw

MR. WHITE

Listen to the wind!

Mr. White exaggeratedly gestures to the window hoping to draw Herbert's attention from his fatal chess mistake.

HERBERT

I'm listening. (Smiling in realisation)

HERBERT (CONT'D)

Check.

MR. WHITE

I should hardly think he'd come tonight.

HERBERT

Mate. (Smiling broadly)

MR. WHITE

(Suddenly angry) That's the worst thing about living so far out. Of all the beastly, slushy, out of-the way places to live in, this is the worst.

He stands in demonstrative gesture.

MR. WHITE (CONT'D)

Pathway's a bog, and the road's a torrent. Nothing is ever done about it I suppose because only two houses in the road are let, they think it doesn't matter!

Screenplay

MRS WHITE

Never mind dear.

Mrs White neither looks up nor conceals her smile.

MRS WHITE (CONT'D)

Perhaps you'll win the next one.

Mr. White catches a knowing glance between his wife and Herbert. A small guilty grin spreads across his face.

A gate outside bangs noisily.

MR. WHITE

There he is.

CUT TO:

EXT. LABURNAM VILLA. NIGHT

Having closed the wrought iron gate, the cloaked figure trudges along the boggy pathway making his way towards the small cottage, braving the adverse weather. Arriving on the front porch he removes the cape to reveal the epaulets of a tall, burly Sergeant Major. Dressed smartly in uniform, he twists the waxy tips of his mustache and raps on the door.

CUT TO:

INT. SMALL COTTAGE PARLOUR. NIGHT

Mr. White opens the door.

The Monkey's Paw

MR. WHITE

Sergeant Major, you came. I didn't expect...
what, with the weather and all. Welcome.
Come in...if you please.

The Sergeant nods politely and enters removing
his hat as the old man hospitably takes both hat
and cape to hang. Mrs White stands looking at
the Sergeant for a moment and awkwardly coughs.

MR. WHITE (CONT'D)

(With melodramatic introduction) Sergeant
Major Morris.

MORRIS

A pleasure.

The Sergeant Major shakes the hand of each
respectively before taking the proffered seat by
the fire. Mr. White busily gets out his whisky
bottle and tumblers and stands a small copper
kettle on the fire, while Mrs White and Herbert
watch with bright eyes.

FADE TO:

Mr. White, Mrs White, and Herbert sit around the
Sergeant Major, listening with eager interest.
The whiskey bottle is half empty and the Sergeant
Major is relishing in their undivided attention.

CUT TO:

CU. A Horse. It whinny's and snuffs in anticipation before a desolate and barren landscape. We see boots in the stirrups, black and highly polished.

MORRIS VO

Victory comes at a price. At Aliwal, the Sikhs occupied a position four miles long. They were in formation to receive Cavalry. Our orders to break the line came from Sir Harry Smith. This was the job of the Sixteenth Lancers.

CUT TO:

We see an Indo-Chinese Urn sitting on a rustic table before a mud brick wall. As we hear the chorus of hooves in the distance, the Urn begins to shake. As the Hooves thunder past, the Urn rocks violently, falls and shatters.

MORRIS VO (CONT'D)

There is nothing romantic about a cavalry charge. It is all speed and snapping and gristle and screaming. A very ugly business. A very ugly business indeed.

CUT TO:

INT. SMALL COTTAGE PARLOUR. NIGHT (CONT'D)

The Monkey's Paw

MR. WHITE

Indeed. And what of India?

MORRIS

A land of exquisite beauty and imminent danger. Sweeping orange sunsets, jugglers, Fakirs, Holy Magicians, old jungle temples littered with Tigers.

MR. WHITE

(Impressed) Twenty-one years of it.

He nods to his wife and son.

MR. WHITE (CONT'D)

When he went away he was a slip of a youth in the warehouse. Now look at him.

MRS WHITE

He don't seem to have taken much harm. (Flirtatiously)

MR. WHITE

I'd like to go myself! Just to look around a bit. You know.

MORRIS

Better where you are. (Shaking his head)

Screenplay

MR. WHITE

I should like to see those old temples and fakirs and jugglers. What was that you were telling me the other day about a monkey's paw or something? Morris?

MORRIS

(Hastily) Nothing. Least ways nothing worth hearing.

Morris looks to the floor willing the conversation to go elsewhere.

MRS WHITE

Monkey's paw?

MORRIS

(Reluctantly) Well, it's just a bit of what you might call magic, perhaps.

The three listeners lean in urging the Sergeant to elaborate. Mr. White again fills up Morris' glass.

The Monkey's Paw

MORRIS (CONT'D)

To look at, it's just an ordinary little paw, dried to a mummy.

Morris fumbles in his pocket and reveals the shriveled charm. He offers it to Mrs White who grimaces at the thought. Herbert grabs it eagerly to examine, which is in turn grabbed by his father.

MR. WHITE

And what is there special about it?

Mr. White examines it then places it on the table.

MORRIS

It had a spell put on it by an old fakir, a very holy man. He wanted to show that fate ruled people's lives, and that those who interfered with it did so to their sorrow. He put a spell on it so that three separate men could each have three wishes from it.

HERBERT

Well why don't you have three, sir? (Cleverly)

There is a long pause. Morris clears his throat, his eyes glistening.

MORRIS

I have.

Screenplay

MRS WHITE

And did you really have the three wishes granted?

MORRIS

I did.

MRS WHITE

And has anybody else wished? (Hopefully)

MORRIS

The first man had his three wishes. Yes. I don't know what the first two were, but the third was for death....

CUT TO:

CU of a face, his eyes are wide with terror and his face is deathly white. He is unblinking.

MORRIS VO

That's how I got the paw.

CUT TO:

INT. COTTAGE PARLOUR. NIGHT (CONT'D)

A hush falls upon the group reflecting Morris' grave tone. A long silence ensues.

The Monkey's Paw

MR. WHITE

If you've had your three wishes it's no good to you now Morris. What do you keep it for?

MORRIS

(Shaking his head) ...I don't know. I don't know. I did have some idea of selling it but I don't think I will. It has caused enough mischief already. Besides, people won't buy. They think it's a fairy tale; some of them, and those who do think anything of it want to try it first and pay me afterward.

MR. WHITE

If you could have another three wishes, would you have them?

MORRIS

I don't know. I don't know.

Morris takes the paw and dangles it between his forefinger and thumb. Suddenly he throws it upon the fire. Mr. White lets out a cry and stoops down snatching it off the flames

MORRIS (CONT'D)

Better to let it burn.

Mr. White inspects the paw for any burns.

Screenplay

MR. WHITE

If you don't want it, Morris, give it to me.

MORRIS

I won't. I threw it on the fire. If you keep it, don't blame me for what happens. Pitch it on the fire again like a sensible man.

MR. WHITE

(Looking closely at the paw) How do you do it?

MORRIS

Hold it up in your right hand and wish aloud. But I warn you of the consequences.

MRS WHITE

Sounds like Arabian Nights!

Mrs White rises and begins to set the supper table.

MRS WHITE (CONT'D)

Don't you think you might wish for four pairs of hands for me?

Mr. White draws the talisman from his pocket and the three family members burst into laughter. Sergeant Major Morris is urgently alarmed and catches Mr. White firmly by the arm. There is a fire in Morris' eyes

MORRIS

You understand very little. If you must wish... wish for something sensible.

Mr. White smiles and drops the paw back into his pocket and placing chairs around the table, ushers his friend towards supper.

FADE TO:

INT. COTTAGE PARLOUR. NIGHT (CONT'D)

Later. The mood has lightened, and laughter is heard as Sergeant Major Morris thanks his hosts, takes his coat and hat and departs in time to make the last train. He vanishes into the rainy night.

HERBERT

(Smiling) I'm afraid if the tale about the monkey's paw is not more truthful than those he has been telling us, we won't make much money out of it.

MRS WHITE

Did you give him anything for it, father?

MR. WHITE

(Embarrassed) A little. He didn't want it, but I made him take it. And he pressed me again to throw it away.

Screenplay

HERBERT

(Pretending horror) Likely! Why we're going to be rich, and famous and happy. Wish to be an Emperor, father, to begin with, then you can't be henpecked.

Mrs. White takes exception to this joke and begins to chase Herbert around the room raising a broomstick propped against the wall. Both begin laughing.

MR. WHITE

I don't know what to wish for, and that's a fact. It seems to me I've got all I want.

Herbert stops, catching his breath and places his hand upon his father's shoulder with feigned sincerity.

HERBERT

If you only cleared the house, you'd be quite happy wouldn't you? Well wish for two hundred pounds then, that'll just do it.

Herbert, still solemn faced, winks at this mother as his father, moved by his son's sincere concern raises the talisman.

MR. WHITE

I wish for two hundred pounds.

A bird screeches from outside and there is a shuddering cry from the old man who has dropped the paw. Mrs. White runs to his side, sharing Herbert's concern.

MR. WHITE (CONT'D)

It moved! As I wished, it twisted in my hand like a snake.

Herbert picks up the talisman and places it on the table, indignant at his father's overreaction.

HERBERT

Well I don't see the money. And I bet I never shall.

MRS WHITE

(Anxiously) It must have been your imagination, father.

MR. WHITE

(Shaking his head) Never mind, though; there's no harm done. But it gave me a shock all the same.

FADE TO:

INT. COTTAGE FIREPLACE. NIGHT

It is later in the evening, the fire is dying, burning low amidst the glowing embers. Mr. White and Herbert sit smoking pipes, alone by the fire lit only by the occasional flame. Outside the wind howls. A clock ticks and the old man jumps at the sound of a door banging upstairs. There is a long silence adding to the air of depression.

Screenplay

HERBERT

I expect you'll find cash tied up in a big bag in the middle of your bed.

Herbert stands as he bids his father goodnight.

HERBERT (CONT'D)

(Smiling) And something horrible squatting up on top of the wardrobe watching you as you pocket your ill-gotten gains.

Herbert departs, but the old man does not return his smile as he sits alone in the darkness. He gazes deep into the fire

CUT TO:

The gaunt white face we saw earlier resembling death. Again the eyes are open wide shocking and silent, we close in on the eyes as if entering into this nightmare.

CUT TO:

The old man startles, struggling for breath. He is clearly shaken and reaches to the nearby table for the jug of water. He accidently grabs the monkey's paw instead and shudders. Upon reaching the jug, he throws the water over the fire, wipes his hand on his coat and leaves for bed.

FADE TO BLACK.

The Monkey's Paw

EXT. LABURNAM VILLA. MORNING

The storm has given way and the winter sun struggles to make its way through the remnant clouds. We see the barren landscape surrounding the quaint cottage. The atmosphere remains grey and bleak.

CUT TO:

INT. BREAKFAST TABLE. MORNING

There is an air of prosaic wholesomeness about the room as Mr. White, Mrs White and Herbert sit to breakfast.

The shriveled monkey's paw is carelessly pitched on the sideboard suggesting none of the macabre potency of the night before.

MRS WHITE

I suppose all old soldiers are the same. The idea of our listening to such nonsense! How could wishes be granted? And if they could, how could two hundred pounds hurt you father?

HERBERT

Might drop on his head from the sky.

The two laugh out loud and even Mr. White seems to have dismissed the terror of the night before as the concoction of imagination and whiskey.

Screenplay

MR. WHITE

Morris said the things happened so naturally, that you might wish to attribute it to coincidence.

HERBERT

Well, don't break into the money before I come back. I'm afraid it will turn you into a mean, greedy man, and we shall have to disown you.

Mrs White laughs as she sees Herbert to the door and watches him down the road. Returning to the breakfast table she hears another knock at the door. She glances at Mr. White and scurries back to the door. The postman smiles, hands her an envelope and departs. Tearing it open, the anticipation is palpable.

MRS WHITE

A bill.

She smiles a little embarrassed at the revelation of her hypocrisy.

MRS WHITE (CONT'D)

A bill from the tailor. I expect we should forward this to Sergeant Major Morris in payment for his entertaining fairy stories.

The Monkey's Paw

                                    FADE TO:

INT. DINNER TABLE. AFTERNOON

Mrs White is preparing the table for dinner. She moves to and from the kitchen bringing crockery and cutlery setting it around Mr. White who sits at the table perusing the tailor's bill.

                MRS WHITE

    Herbert will have some more of his funny remarks, I expect, when he comes home from the factory.

Mr. White smiles in agreement and places the bill on the table.

                MR. WHITE

    I dare say. But for all that, the thing moved in my hand; that I'll swear to.

                MRS WHITE

    You thought it did. That is all.

                MR. WHITE

    I say it did. There was no thought about it; I had just....

Mrs White's attention is caught by something outside the window and she moves towards it.

Screenplay

> MR. WHITE (CONT'D)
>
> What's the matter?

CUT TO:

EXT. LABURNAM VILLA. AFTERNOON

A well-dressed gentleman wearing a silk hat of glossy newness walks towards the house gate and at the last moment continues past before pausing and repeating the process in the other direction. This is repeated a third time in an undecided fashion before finally with resolution he puts his hand on the gate, flings it open and walks up the path.

CUT TO:

INT. COTTAGE PARLOUR. AFTERNOON

Without answering her husband, Mrs White unfastens her apron strings and places it beneath the cushion of her chair. She walks carefully towards the door as the first knock sounds, trying not to get ahead of herself mentally connecting the two hundred pounds.

She opens the door.

> GENTLEMAN
>
> Good day madam. May I come in?

Mrs White opens the door politely and gestures him into the room, she is embarrassed at the state of the parlour.

The Monkey's Paw

MRS WHITE

Please do come in. I do apologise Sir, we were not expecting guests. Mr. White has been gardening. He would never commonly be in this attire..

There is a long silence.

GENTLEMAN

I... was asked to call.... I come from Maw and Meggins.

MRS WHITE

Is anything the matter? (Breathlessly) Has anything happened to Herbert? What is it? What is it?

MR. WHITE

There, there mother. Sit down and don't jump to conclusions. You've not brought bad news, I'm sure sir.

GENTLEMAN

I'm sorry.

MRS WHITE

Is he hurt?

The gentleman bows awkwardly in assent.

Screenplay

                    GENTLEMAN

   Badly hurt...

There is a long pause.

                  GENTLEMAN (CONT'D)

   But he is not in any pain.

                      MRS WHITE

   Oh, thank God... Thank God for that! Thank....

Realising the gentleman's implications, she
sees the awful confirmation of her fears in his
anguished face. Catching her breath, she turns to
her slower witted husband and lays her trembling
hands upon his. There is a long silence.

                      GENTLEMAN

   He was caught in the machinery.

                      MR. WHITE

   Caught in the machinery. (Dazed)

   Yes.

Mr. White sits looking blankly out of the window
and presses his wife's hand between his own. His
words are hard to find

                  MR. WHITE (CONT'D)

   He was the only one left to us... it is hard.

The Monkey's Paw

The gentleman coughs and walks slowly to the window.

GENTLEMAN

The firm wished me to convey their sincere sympathy with you in your great loss. I beg that you will understand I am only their servant and merely obeying orders.

There is no reply. Both Mr. and Mrs White stand wide eyed, breathless and pale.

GENTLEMAN (CONT'D)

I was to say that Maw and Meggins disclaim all responsibility. They admit no liability at all, but in consideration of your son's services, they wish to present you with a certain sum as compensation.

Mr. White drops his wife's hand and rises to his feet with a look of horror.

MR. WHITE

How much?

GENTLEMAN

Two hundred pounds.

There is a shrill scream from Mrs White. Mr. White puts out his hands like a blind man and drops senseless to the floor

FADE TO
BLACK

EXT. CEMETARY.DAY

The scene is bleak and grey at the cemetery as Mr. White looks down into the freshly dug hole, the coffin sitting lifeless at the base. He is pale and gaunt and finally bends down, picks up a mound of earth and throws it on the coffin

WHITE FLASH

CUT

CU of same pale haunting face from earlier. The eyes are wide and bloodshot, decay is evident around the orbits. We hear a barely audible whisper.

WHISPER

Two hundred pounds....

CUT TO:

INT. COTTAGE BEDROOM. NIGHT

Mr. White sits bolt upright in his bed with a startled breath. We see the vapor as he regains his breath in the icy air. His face is hopeful, perhaps it was a dream? He clambers out of bed and makes his way into Herbert's room. But as he gazes at the empty bed in the darkness, reality realises his fears. At the bedroom window stands his wife, staring into the darkness blankly.

MR. WHITE

Come back to bed. You will be cold.

MRS WHITE

It is colder for my son. Gone ten days. It is colder for my son.

Mrs White again begins weeping and Mr. White helplessly returns to his bed.

CUT TO:

INT. COTTAGE BEDROOM. NIGHT

Mr. White is finally sound asleep in his bed when Mrs White bursts through the door waking him with a start.

MRS WHITE

The paw! The monkey's paw!

MR. WHITE

(Alarmed) Where? Where is it? What's the matter?

Mrs White stumbles across the room towards him.

MRS WHITE

I want it. You've not destroyed it?

Screenplay

MR. WHITE

It's in the parlour, on the bracket. Why?

Mrs White begins laughing and crying together and bends kissing his cheek.

MRS WHITE

(Hysterically) I only just thought of it. Why didn't I think of it before? Why didn't you think of it?

MR. WHITE

Think of what?

MRS WHITE

The other two wishes? We've only had one.

MR. WHITE

(Fiercely) Was that not enough?

MRS WHITE

No. We'll have one more. Go down and get it quickly, and wish our boy alive again.

Mr. White sits up throwing the blanket from his shaking limbs.

MR. WHITE

Good God, you are mad!

The Monkey's Paw

MRS WHITE

Get it! Get it quickly and wish...Oh my boy, my boy!

Mr. White strikes a match and lights a candle.

MR. WHITE

Get back to bed. You don't know what you are saying.

MRS WHITE

We had the first wish granted. Why not the second?

MR. WHITE

A coincidence.

MRS WHITE

Go and get it and wish.

The old man slowly turns towards her, his voice quivers.

MR. WHITE

He has been dead ten days. And besides he...I cannot tell you more... I had to identify him. I could only recognise him by his clothing. If he was too terrible for you to see then, how now?

Screenplay

MRS WHITE

Bring him back.

Mrs White becomes instantly fierce and drags her husband to the door.

MRS WHITE (CONT'D)

Do you think I would fear the child I have nursed?

CUT TO:

INT. STAIR PASSAGE/ COTTAGE PARLOUR. NIGHT (CONT'D)

Mr. White, descends down the stairs into the darkness, feeling his way into the parlour and then to the mantelpiece. The Talisman is in its place. As he grasps the paw, his breath is sharp and pained. After a long pause he again feels his way around the table and back to the stairwell.

CUT TO:

INT. COTTAGE BEDROOM. NIGHT

Mrs White stands beside the bed as her husband re enters. Her face is white, expectant and unnatural. Mr. White is afraid of her.

MRS WHITE

Wish!

The Monkey's Paw

MR. WHITE

It is foolish and wicked.

MRS WHITE

Wish! (Forceful)

Mr. White slowly raises his trembling hand.

MR. WHITE

I wish my son alive again.

The Talisman falls to the floor as Mr. White sinks trembling into a chair. Mrs White moves to the window and raises the blind.

The old man stands with his candle trembling in the dark. The candle flickers, pulsating shadows on the ceiling and walls. Every breath the old man takes, steams in the cold as he watches his wife, old and frail at the window. Time seems to pass so slowly. A clock ticks rhythmically and we hear the exaggerated breathing. Finally after a long silence, the candle expires in a thin stream of smoke. Nothing.

A look of relief appears on Mr. White's face. Resolved he climbs back into the cold bed. A moment later and Mrs White silently climbs in beside him, her despair is great.

As they lay in silence, in darkness, we hear the ticking clock, a stair creaks and a mouse scurries noisily through the wall.

Screenplay

MR. WHITE (CONT'D)

(Whispering) I'll get a candle.

He climbs out of bed and taking the box of matches by his bedside table, strikes a match. In the dim light he goes downstairs to get a candle.

CUT TO:

INT. STAIR PASSAGE. NIGHT (CONT'D)

At the foot of the stairs, Mr. White's match goes out and he pauses to strike another. There is a quiet, barely audible knock on the front door. The match falls from his hand and spills in the passage. For a moment he stands motionless, his breath suspended.

The knock repeats.

He turns and returns swiftly to his room in the dark. Closing the door behind him.

CUT TO:

INT. COTTAGE BEDROOM. NIGHT

A third knock sounds through the house.

MRS WHITE

What's that?

MR. WHITE

A ra...rat. It passed me on the stairs.

The Monkey's Paw

Mrs White sits up in bed. A knock again resounds through the house.

MRS WHITE

It's Herbert! It's Herbert!

Mrs White runs to the door, Mr. White grabs her arm firmly and holds her tightly

MR. WHITE

(Hoarsely) What are you going to do?

MRS WHITE

It's my boy; it's Herbert! I forgot the cemetery was two miles away. What are you holding me for? Let go. I must open the door.

MR. WHITE

For God's sake don't let it in!

MRS WHITE

You're afraid of your own son? Let me go. I'm coming Herbert; I'm coming.

There is another knock and another. The old woman wrenches herself free and runs from the room. Mr. White follows her to the landing pleading.

Screenplay

MR. WHITE

You don't understand what you are doing.

We hear the chain on the front door rattle back and the bottom bolt drawn stiffly from the socket

MRS WHITE VO

(Straining) The bolt. Come down. I can't reach it.

Mr. White drops on his hands and knees, groping wildly on the floor in search of the paw

We hear continual knocking and a chair being scraped across the floor in the parlour. The bolt creaks as it is being drawn slowly back.

Mr. White's hand fumbles across the monkey's paw and he grasps it tightly.

MR. WHITE

I wish....

CUT TO:

INT. COTTAGE PARLOUR. NIGHT

The knocking stops.

Mrs White draws the chair back and opens the door. Nothing. A wind rushes through the door. Mrs White wails from misery and flops to the floor. In a moment Mr. White is by her side. He puts a hand on her shoulder tenderly before looking to the gate beyond.

A street lamp flickering opposite shines on a quiet and deserted road.

HOW TO READ A GRAPHIC NOVEL

Reading a graphic novel or a comic is an important literacy skill to have. The significant difference between a graphic novel and the scripts presented in this book are the combination of pictures and text at the same time. This is the first golden rule when reading a graphic novel; the image and the text need to be absorbed at the same time. They inform one another, the picture adds information to the text.

Just like any book you would read in western society, you start at the top left. It should be noted however that Manga comic, just like Japanese writing, starts at the top right. The first box, referred to as a "panel" contains a combination of pictures and text, which need to be considered as a whole. Take time to appreciate the full meaning of the panel before moving on. Generally you move across the page to the right then down to the next panel, just as you would with a book. Occasionally you may come across a page which does not use formal panels. The best idea is to drag a ruler down the page stopping after each element and reading from left to right.

When a character in a panel speaks, it is usually indicated by a speech bubble tail that points to the character. Sometimes the character's speech may continue into the next panel as the story builds.

You may also notice that there seems to be some words misspelt such as "Nok". In the world of comics, sounds are phonetic. In other words, a noise is written exactly as it sounds.

In comics, everything has meaning. Everything. Not just the composition of each panel and the choices of size and angles, but also the layout. Take time to try and find the meaning behind each choice and let the story reveal itself.

THE MONKEY'S PAW

GRAPHIC NOVEL

A. KELLY

The Monkey's Paw

The Monkey's Paw

Graphic Novel

The Monkey's Paw

The Monkey's Paw

The Monkey's Paw

66

The Monkey's Paw

HOW TO READ A STAGE PLAY

Just like a movie, a stage play is divided into scenes. These are numbered and indicated in the centre of the page. These scenes are collected into larger groups or parts called an "Act". "The Monkey's Paw" is a one Act play, but longer plays can have as many as five. Beneath the scene number -centred right- is a description of what we see on stage at the beginning of the scene.

When there is a centred character's name in capital letters, it is followed by dialogue by that character.

e.g.
MR. WHITE

Listen to the wind!

If there are words in brackets in the dialogue, this is a direction for the characters performance.

e.g.
HERBERT

I'm listening. (Smiling in realisation)

Whenever there is stage direction for a character, it is written centred right.

e.g.   Mr. White exaggeratedly gestures to the window hoping to draw Herbert's attention from his fatal chess mistake.

The changing of a scene is usually indicated with a lighting direction e.g.

LIGHTS UP
LIGHTS DOWN

A play always makes more sense by reading and trying to act it out. Try to allocate an actor for each character and someone to read the stage directions initially. In the actual performance of the story, there will be no need to read the stage directions as the actors will simply do what is directed in the script and the set and props will hopefully set the scene.

THE MONKEY'S PAW
STAGE PLAY

ADAPTED BY
SHANE EMMETT

BASED ON THE STORY BY W.W. JACOBS

Stage Play

The Players

- Mr. White

- Mrs White

- Herbert White

- Sergeant Major Morris

- Gentleman

The Monkey's Paw

ACT 1.

> SCENE 1.
>
> Inside a rustic cottage parlour. A fire crackles in a modest hearth offering little light and warmth. We hear the rain pounding and the wind howling outside the window. An old man, Mr. White sits opposite his son, Herbert White passing the time playing chess on a rustic table. Closer to the fire sits Mrs White, a white haired old lady knitting placidly.

> MR. WHITE

Listen to the wind!

> Mr. White exaggeratedly gestures to the window hoping to draw Herbert's attention from his fatal chess mistake.

> HERBERT

I'm listening. (Smiling in realisation)

> HERBERT (CONT'D)

Check.

Stage Play

MR. WHITE

I should hardly think he'd come tonight.

HERBERT

Mate. (Smiling broadly)

MR. WHITE

(Suddenly angry) That's the worst thing about living so far out. Of all the beastly, slushy, out-of-the way places to live in, this is the worst.

> He stands in a demonstrative gesture.

MR. WHITE (CONT'D)

Pathway's a bog, and the road's a torrent. Nothing is ever done about it I suppose because only two houses in the road are let, they think it doesn't matter!

MRS WHITE

Never mind dear.

> Mrs White neither looks up nor conceals her smile.

MRS WHITE (CONT'D)

Perhaps you'll win the next one.

Mr. White catches a knowing glance between his wife and Herbert. A small guilty grin spreads across his face.

A gate outside bangs noisily.

MR. WHITE

There he is.

Mr. White rises at the sound of a rap at the door. He opens the door to reveal a tall, burly Sergeant Major. Dressed smartly in uniform, cape removed, twisting the waxy tips of his mustache.

MR. WHITE

Sergeant Major, you came. I didn't expect... what with the weather and all... Welcome. Come in... if you please.

The Sergeant nods politely and enters removing his hat as the old man hospitably takes both hat and cape to hang. Mrs White stands looking at the Sergeant for a moment and awkwardly coughs.

Stage Play

MR. WHITE (CONT'D)

(Realising with melodramatic introduction)
Sergeant Major Morris.

MORRIS

A pleasure.

The Sergeant Major shakes the hand of each respectively before taking the proffered seat by the fire. Mr. White busily gets out his whisky bottle and tumblers and stands a small copper kettle on the fire, while Mrs White and Herbert watch with bright eyes.

LIGHTS DOWN

We hear the ticking of a clock which fades.

LIGHTS UP

> Mr. White, Mrs White, and Herbert sit around the Sergeant Major, listening with eager interest. The whiskey bottle is half empty and the Sergeant-Major is relishing in their undivided attention.

MORRIS

Victory comes at a price. At Aliwal, the Sikhs occupied a position four miles long. They were in formation to receive Cavalry. Our orders to break the line came from Sir Harry Smith. This was the job of the Sixteenth Lancers. There is nothing romantic about a cavalry charge. It is all speed and snapping and gristle and screaming. A very ugly business. A very ugly business indeed.

MR. WHITE

Indeed. And what of India?

MORRIS

A land of exquisite beauty and imminent danger. Sweeping orange sunsets, jugglers, Fakirs, Holy Magicians, old jungle temples littered with Tigers.

Stage Play

MR. WHITE

(Impressed) Twenty-one years of it. (He nods to his wife and son.) When he went away he was a slip of a youth in the warehouse. Now look at him.

MRS WHITE

He don't seem to have taken much harm. (Flirtatiously)

MR. WHITE

I'd like to go myself! Just to look around a bit. You know.

MORRIS

Better where you are. (Shaking his head)

MR. WHITE

I should like see those old temples and fakirs and Jugglers. What was that you were telling me the other day about a monkey's paw or something, Morris?

MORRIS

(Hastily) Nothing. Leastways nothing worth hearing.

> Morris looks to the floor willing the conversation to go elsewhere.

The Monkey's Paw

MRS WHITE

Monkey's paw?

MORRIS

(Reluctantly) Well, it's just a bit of what you might call magic, perhaps.

> The three listeners lean in, urging the Sergeant to elaborate. Mr. White again fills up Morris' glass

MORRIS (CONT'D)

To look at, it's just an ordinary little paw, dried to a mummy.

> Morris fumbles in his pocket and reveals the shrivelled charm. He offers it to Mrs White who grimaces at the thought. Herbert grabs it eagerly to examine, which is in turn grabbed by his father.

MR. WHITE

And what is there special about it?

> Mr. White examines it then places it on the table.

MORRIS

It had a spell put on it by an old fakir, a very holy man. He wanted to show that fate ruled people's lives, and that those who interfered with it did so to their sorrow. He put a spell on it so that three separate men could each have three wishes from it.

HERBERT

Well why don't you have three, sir? (Cleverly)

> There is a long pause.
> Morris clears his throat,
> his eyes glistening.

MORRIS

I have.

MRS WHITE

And did you really have the three wishes granted?

MORRIS

I did.

MRS WHITE

And has anybody else wished? (Hopefully)

The Monkey's Paw

MORRIS

The first man had his three wishes. Yes. I don't know what the first two were, but the third was for death.... That's how I got the paw.

> A hush falls upon the group reflecting Morris' grave tone. A long silence ensues.

MR. WHITE

If you've had your three wishes, it's no good to you now then Morris. What do you keep it for?

MORRIS

(Shaking his head) ...I don't know. I don't know. I did have some idea of selling it but I don't think I will. It has caused enough mischief already. Besides, people won't buy. They think it's a fairy tale; some of them, and those who do think anything of it want to try it first and pay me afterward.

MR. WHITE

If you could have another three wishes, would you have them?

Stage Play

MORRIS

I don't know. I don't know.

> Morris takes the paw and dangles it between his forefinger and thumb. Suddenly he throws it upon the fire. Mr. White lets out a cry and stoops down snatching it off the flames

MORRIS (CONT'D)

Better let it burn.

> Mr. White inspects the paw for any burns.

MR. WHITE

If you don't want it Morris, give it to me.

MORRIS

I won't. I threw it on the fire. If you keep it, don't blame me for what happens. Pitch it on the fire again like a sensible man.

MR. WHITE

(Looking closely at the paw) How do you do it?

MORRIS

Hold it up in your right hand and wish aloud. But I warn you of the consequences.

The Monkey's Paw

MRS WHITE

Sounds like Arabian Nights!

> Mrs White rises and begins
> to set the supper table.

MRS WHITE (CONT'D)

Don't you think you might wish for four pairs of hands for me?

> Mr. White draws the talisman
> from his pocket and the
> three family members burst
> into laughter. Sergeant
> Major Morris is urgently
> alarmed and catches Mr.
> White firmly by the arm.
> There is a fire in Morris'
> eyes.

MORRIS

You understand very little. If you must wish.... wish for something sensible.

> Mr. White smiles and drops
> the paw back into his pocket
> and placing chairs around
> the table, ushers his friend
> towards supper.

LIGHTS DOWN

> The ticking of a clock is
> heard and fades.

Stage Play

LIGHTS UP

> It is later, the mood has lightened, and laughter is heard as Sergeant Major Morris thanks his hosts, takes his coat and hat and departs in time to make the last train. He exits through the front door.

HERBERT

(Smiling) I'm afraid if the tale about the Monkey's paw is not more truthful than those he has been telling us, we won't make much money out if it.

MRS WHITE

Did you give him anything for it, father?

MR. WHITE

(Embarrassed) A little. He didn't want it, but I made him take it. And he pressed me again to throw it away.

The Monkey's Paw

HERBERT

(Pretending horror) Likely! Why we're going to be rich, and famous and happy. Wish to be an Emperor, father, to begin with; then you can't be henpecked.

> Mrs White takes exception to this joke and begins to chase Herbert around the room raising a broomstick that is propped against the wall. Both begin laughing.

MR. WHITE

I don't know what to wish for, and that's a fact. It seems to me I've got all I want.

> Herbert stops, catching his breath and places his hand upon his father's shoulder with feigned sincerity.

HERBERT

If you only cleared the house, you'd be quite happy wouldn't you? Well wish for two hundred pounds then, that'll just do it.

> Herbert still solemn faced, winks at his mother as his father, moved by his son's sincere concern raises the talisman.

Stage Play

MR. WHITE

I wish for two hundred pounds.

> A bird screeches from outside and there is a shuddering cry from the old man who has dropped the paw. Mrs White runs to his side, sharing Herbert's concern.

MR. WHITE (CONT'D)

It moved! As I wished, it twisted in my hand like a snake.

> Herbert picks up the talisman and places it on the table, indignant at his father's overreaction.

HERBERT

Well I don't see the money. And I bet I never shall.

MRS WHITE

(Anxiously) It must have been your imagination, father.

MR. WHITE

(Shaking his head) Never mind, though; there's no harm done. But it gave me a shock all the same.

LIGHTS DOWN

SCENE 2.

It is later in the evening, the fire is dying, burning low amidst the glowing embers. Mr. White and Herbert sit smoking pipes, alone by the fire in the dim flickering light. Outside the wind howls. A clock ticks and the old man jumps at the sound of a door banging upstairs. There is a long silence adding to the air of depression.

HERBERT

I expect you'll find cash tied up in a big bag in the middle of your bed.

Herbert stands as he bids his father goodnight.

Stage Play

HERBERT (CONT'D)

(Smiling) And something horrible squatting up on top of the wardrobe watching you as you pocket your ill-gotten gains.

> Herbert departs and climbs the stairs to the bedrooms, but the old man does not return his smile as he sits alone in the darkness. He gazes deep into the fire. There is a long silence until subtle sounds, moaning, crackling, howling, laughing, grow into a crescendo. The old man startles, struggling for breath. He is clearly shaken and reaches to the nearby table for the jug of water. He accidently grabs the Monkey paw instead and shudders. Upon reaching the jug, he throws the water over the fire, wipes his hand on his coat and leaves for bed.

LIGHTS DOWN

The Monkey's Paw

SCENE 3.

It is morning. The wind and rain has abated, and although the room appears bleak and gloomy, there is an air of wholesomeness about the room as Mr. White, Mrs White and Herbert sit to breakfast at the table. The shrivelled Monkey's paw is carelessly pitched on the sideboard suggesting none of the macabre potency of the night before.

MRS WHITE

I suppose all old soldiers are the same. The idea of our listening to such nonsense! How could wishes be granted? And if they could, how could two hundred pounds hurt you father?

HERBERT

Might drop on his head from the sky.

The two laugh out loud and even Mr. White seems to have dismissed the terror of the night before.

MR. WHITE

Morris said the things happened so naturally, that you might wish to attribute it to coincidence.

Stage Play

HERBERT

Well, don't break into the money before I come back. I'm afraid it will turn you into a mean, greedy man, and we shall have to disown you.

> Mrs White laughs as she sees Herbert to the door.

MRS WHITE

You have a nice day love.

> She watches him walk down the road. Returning to the breakfast table she hears another knock at the door. She glances at Mr. White and scurries back to the door. The postman smiles, hands her an envelope and departs. Tearing it open, the anticipation is palpable.

MRS WHITE

A bill.

> She smiles a little embarrassed at the revelation of her hypocrisy.

MRS WHITE (CONT'D)

A bill from the tailor. I expect we should forward this to Sergeant-Major Morris in payment for his entertaining fairy stories.

LIGHTS DOWN

The Monkey's Paw

SCENE 4.

It is later in the day and Mrs White is preparing the table for dinner. She moves to and from the kitchen bringing crockery and cutlery setting it around Mr. White who wears the remnants of a day gardening but now sits at the table perusing the tailor's bill.

MRS WHITE

Herbert will have some more of his funny remarks, I expect, when he comes home from the factory.

Mr. White smiles in agreement and places the bill on the table.

MR. WHITE

I dare say. But for all that, the thing moved in my hand; that I'll swear to.

MRS WHITE

You thought it did. That is all.

MR. WHITE

I say it did. There was no thought about it; I had just....

Stage Play

> Mrs White's attention is caught by something outside the window and she moves towards it.

MR. WHITE (CONT'D)

What's the matter?

> Without answering her husband, Mrs White unfastens her apron strings and places it beneath the cushion of her chair. She walks carefully towards the door as the first knock sounds, trying not to get ahead of herself.
>
> She opens the door to reveal a well dressed gentleman wearing a silk hat of glossy newness which he duly removes courteously.

GENTLEMAN

Good day madam. May I come in?

> Mrs White opens the door politely and gestures him into the room, she is embarrassed at the state of the parlour.

The Monkey's Paw

MRS WHITE

Please do come in. I do apologise Sir, we were not expecting guests. Mr. White has been gardening. He would never commonly be in this attire..

> There is a long silence.

GENTLEMAN

I... was asked to call.... I come from Maw and Meggins.

MRS WHITE

Is anything the matter? (Breathlessly) Has anything happened to Herbert? What is it? What is it?

MR. WHITE

There, there mother. Sit down and don't jump to conclusions. You've not brought bad news, I'm sure sir.

GENTLEMAN

I'm sorry.

MRS WHITE

Is he hurt?

> The gentleman bows awkwardly in assent.

Stage Play

GENTLEMAN

Badly hurt... (There is a long pause). But he is not in any pain.

MRS WHITE

Oh, thank God.. Thank God for that! Thank.....

> Realising the gentleman's implications, she sees the awful confirmation of her fears in his anguished face. Catching her breath, she turns to her slower witted husband and lays her trembling hands upon his. There is a long silence.

GENTLEMAN

He was caught in the machinery.

MR. WHITE

Caught in the machinery.(Dazed) Yes.

> Mr. White sits looking blankly out of the window and presses his wife's hand between his own. His words are hard to find

The Monkey's Paw

MR. WHITE (CONT'D)

He was the only one left to us... it is hard.

> The gentleman coughs and walks slowly to the window.

GENTLEMAN

The firm wished me to convey their sincere sympathy with you in your great loss. I beg that you will understand I am only their servant and merely obeying orders.

> There is no reply. Both Mr. and Mrs White stand wide-eyed, breathless and pale.

GENTLEMAN (CONT'D)

I was to say that Maw and Meggins disclaim all responsibility. They admit no liability at all, but in consideration of your son's services, they wish to present you with a certain sum as compensation.

> Mr. White drops his wife's hand and rises to his feet gazing with a look of horror.

MR. WHITE

How much?

GENTLEMAN

Two hundred pounds.

Stage Play

There is a shrill scream from Mrs White. Mr. White puts out his hands like a blind man and drops senseless to the floor

LIGHTS DOWN

SCENE 6.

In the upstairs bedroom, Mr. White is asleep in his bed alone. Mr. White suddenly sits bolt upright in his bed with a startled breath. The wind again is howling outside. His face is hopeful, perhaps it was a dream? He clambers out of bed and makes his way into Herbert's room. But as he gazes at the empty bed in the darkness, reality realises his fears. At the bedroom window stands his wife, staring into the darkness blankly.

MR. WHITE

Come back to bed. You will be cold.

The Monkey's Paw

MRS WHITE

It is colder for my son. Gone ten days. It is colder for my son.

> Mrs White again begins weeping and Mr. White helplessly returns to his bed where he tosses and turns for a time and finally falls asleep. Mrs White suddenly bursts through the door waking him with a start.

MRS WHITE

The paw! The monkey's Paw!

MR. WHITE

(Alarmed) Where? Where is it? What's the matter?

> Mrs White stumbles across the room towards him.

MRS WHITE

I want it. You've not destroyed it?

MR. WHITE

It's in the parlour, on the bracket? Why?

> Mrs White begins laughing and crying together and bends kissing his cheek.

Stage Play

MRS WHITE

(Hysterically) I only just thought if it. Why didn't I think of it before? Why didn't you think of it?

MR. WHITE

Think of what?

MRS WHITE

The other two wishes? We've only had one.

MR. WHITE

(Fiercely) Was that not enough?

MRS WHITE

No. We'll have one more. Go down and get it quickly, and wish our boy alive again.

> Mr. White sits up throwing the blanket from his shaking limbs.

MR. WHITE

Good God, you are mad!

MRS WHITE

Get it! Get it quickly and wish...Oh my boy, my boy!

The Monkey's Paw

> Mr. White strikes a match and lights a candle.

MR. WHITE

Get back to bed. You don't know what you are saying.

MRS WHITE

We had the first wish granted. Why not the second?

MR. WHITE

A coincidence.

MRS WHITE

Go and get it and wish.

> The old man slowly turns towards her, his voice quivers.

MR. WHITE

He has been dead ten days. And besides he...I can not tell you else.. I had to identify him. I could only recognise him by his clothing. If he was too terrible for you to see then, how now?

MRS WHITE

Bring him back.

Stage Play

> Mrs White becomes instantly fierce and drags her husband to the door.

MRS WHITE (CONT'D)

Do you think I would fear the child I have nursed?

> Mr. White reluctantly exits the room and descends down the stairs into the darkness, feeling his way into the parlour and then to the mantelpiece. The Talisman is in it's place. As he grasps the paw, his breath is sharp and pained. After a long pause he again feels his way around the table and back to the stairwell.
>
> Mrs White stands beside the bed as her husband re-enters. Her face is white, expectant and unnatural. Mr. White is afraid of her.

MRS WHITE

Wish!

MR. WHITE

It is foolish and wicked.

The Monkey's Paw

MRS WHITE

Wish! (Forceful)

Mr. White slowly raises his trembling hand.

MR. WHITE

I wish my son alive again.

The Talisman falls to the floor as M. White sinks trembling into a chair. Mrs White moves to the window and raises the blind.

The old man stands with his candle trembling in the dark, breathing heavily in the cold as he watches his wife, old and frail at the window. Time seems to pass so slowly. A clock ticks rhythmically. Finally after a long silence, the candle goes out.

MR. WHITE

Nothing!

A look of relief appears on Mr. White's face. Resolved he climbs back into the cold bed. A moment later and Mrs White silently climbs in beside him, her despair is great.

Stage Play

> As they lay in silence, in darkness, we hear the ticking clock, a stair creaks and a mouse scurries noisily through the wall.

                    MR. WHITE (CONT'D)
(Whispering) I'll get a candle.

> He climbs out of bed and taking the box of matches by his bedside table, strikes a match. In the dim light he goes downstairs to get a candle.
>
> At the foot of the stairs, Mr. White's match goes out and he pauses to strike another. There is a quiet, barely audible knock on the front door. The match falls from his hand and spills in the passage. For a moment he stands motionless, his breath suspended.
>
> The knock repeats.
>
> He turns and returns swiftly to his room in the dark. Closing the door behind him.
>
> A third knock sounds through the house.

                    MRS WHITE
What's that?

The Monkey's Paw

MR. WHITE

A rat...a rat. It passed me on the stairs.

> Mrs White sits up in bed. A knock again resounds through the house.

MRS WHITE

It's Herbert! It's Herbert!

> Mrs White runs to the door. Mr. White grabs her arm firmly and holds her tightly

MR. WHITE

(Hoarsely) What are you going to do?

MRS WHITE

It's my boy; it's Herbert! I forgot the cemetery was two miles away. What are you holding me for? Let go. I must open the door.

MR. WHITE

For God's sake don't let it in!

Stage Play

MRS WHITE

You're afraid of your own son? Let me go. I'm coming Herbert; I'm coming.

> There is another knock and another. The old woman wrenches herself free and runs from the room. Mr. White follows her to the stairs pleading.

MR. WHITE

You don't understand what you are doing.

> Mrs White rattles back the chain on the front door and tries to draw the bottom bolt from the socket.

MRS WHITE

(Straining) The bolt. Come down. I can't reach it.

> Mr. White drops on his hands and knees, groping wildly on the floor in search of the paw.
>
> We hear continual knocking as Mrs White scrapes a chair across the floor in the parlour. The bolt creaks as she draws it slowly back.
>
> Mr. White's hand fumbles across the Monkey's paw and he grasps it tightly.

The Monkey's Paw

MR. WHITE

I wish Herbert life no more.

The knocking stops.

Mrs White draws the chair back and opens the door. Nothing. A wind rushes through the door. Mrs White wails in misery and flops to the floor. In a moment Mr. White is by her side. He puts a hand on her shoulder tenderly before looking to the gate beyond.

The road is empty and silent

LIGHTS DOWN

THE MONKEY'S PAW
IN THE CLASSROOM

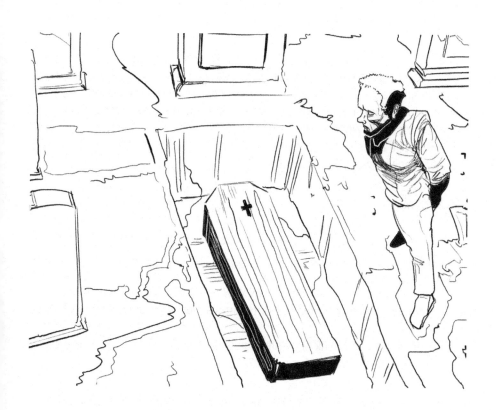

THEMES:

1) The wish and its danger:

Greed is the real cause of grief in this story. Mr. White has all that he needs "I don't know what to wish for...it seems I've got all I want". Yet, he is goaded by his wife and son to wish for more. It is only a seemingly harmless wish "£200", but the consequences are dire. Mrs White, believing the paw's power to be infinite, forces Mr. White to wish for the resurrection of their son. The equation is simple- greed leads to unhappiness. Desire leads to expectations unfulfilled and consequences beyond your control.

Questions:

1. What is a moral tale? Write a closing paragraph highlighting the moral of the story.
2. This story was originally written by W.W Jacobs in 1902. Do you think an audience back then would feel differently about the story than today? Why?
3. What else do you think Mr. White could have wished for? What do you think the consequence might have been?

2) Clash between the domestic and the outside world:

The White's house, "the domestic", is a symbol of safety, warmth and security. It is small, warm and appears an environment of happiness and affection. Each subsequent visitor brings trouble into this harmonious environment, which is a direct result of the invitation of the first visitor. Sergeant Major Morris disrupts this harmony when he brings his stories of the exotic and violent world into the household. He finally gives them the supreme symbol of this dangerous world, the monkey's paw. The Maw and Meggins representative brings news of tragedy and the full revelation of the horror caused by their greed. The final visitor would be Herbert. Mr. White prevents him from entering the home, understanding both the true horror of his appearance and the danger that he poses to the domestic world.

Questions:

1. Try and find as many examples from the text as possible that support the idea that the domestic world is a warm, happy safe world. e.g. copper kettle, fireplace.

2. What are some of the things in your home that make you feel safe and secure?

3) The Supernatural:

The Monkey's Paw is a story where we never really know if there are supernatural forces at work or not. The monkey's paw is either really magic and responsible for Herbert's death and the potential return for the undead, or it is just a shrivelled up totem that isn't magic and Herbert's death and the door knocks are just a coincidence.

Throughout the story, the characters struggle with these exact possibilities. This uncertainty is exactly what W.W Jacobs wanted us to feel over 100 years ago when the story was first written.

Questions:

1. Do you think Mr. White's third and final wish was the right one? Why?

2. How could you re-word Mr. White's final wish to ensure that Herbert didn't return like a decomposed undead corpse?

3. Draw a picture of what you imagine the final visitor looks like as they knock on the door.

4) Fate and Free will:

How much power do we have over the direction of our lives? Are the White's responsible for Herbert's death or are they the victims of events that were always destined to be? There are two schools of thought about events in our lives. "Free will" is the notion that we are in control of what happens in our lives through the choices we make. While "fate" is the notion that the events are all predestined and we are merely players reading the lines to a pre-written play.

The Monkey's Paw explores the idea of choices. Mr. White decides to keep the paw but reluctantly makes the first wish. This reluctance is greater when he makes the second wish against his will because of the will of his wife. Finally Mr. White finds his strength when he makes his final wish, perhaps because he desires to take control of his own life and his choices.

Questions:

1. How do the wishes we make impact the course of our lives?

2. Were Mr. White's wishes always destined to be curses or could he have wished more carefully?

3. Find examples in the text when characters do things against their will.

4. What are your thoughts on fate or free will in your own life?

5) Death:

The loss of a loved one is one of the most difficult events we deal with in life and we see it transform the White family in "The Monkey's Paw". Herbert is their only son and it is natural for them to dwell on how the tragedy could have been prevented. The last part of the story is heavy with grief and guilt. Even without the monkey's paw, Mrs White would have blamed herself for not stopping Herbert going to work that day. For her, death was the worst possible fate. However, for Mr. White, the decomposed, undead corpse of his son would be far worse.

In The Classroom

In 1902 when W.W Jacobs first wrote the story, death, disease and high mortality rates would have been familiar to an audience in industrial revolution England. Deaths related to factory work were excessively high and would have been very relevant to the story's audience.

Questions:

1. If you knew that Herbert had brothers and sisters that had died also, would that change the way you see the Whites? Why?

2. Would you have also made the same third wish as Mr. White? Why? Do you think he made this wish for Herbert's sake or for himself and his wife?

3. What were some of the dangers of living in the early 1900's? What are some of the common causes of death today? What has changed and why?

6) Family:

The White family is the centre of the Monkey's Paw story. We see their jovial love in the opening scenes, which is disrupted by Sergeant Major Morris and the monkey's paw. The wish for no financial debt coincides with the worst possible consequence when Herbert is killed. We see the White's intense grief and genuine love for their son so much that Mrs White wishes him back without caring for the cost.

The Monkey's Paw

Questions:

1. How would you describe the White's family life?

2. Mr. White alludes to the fact that there used to be other White children. We assume they have been able to work through their previous grief with the other children. Do you think they will be able to do the same with Herbert?

3. How would you describe the relationship between:
   - Mr. and Mrs White?
   - Mr. White and Herbert?
   - Mrs White and Herbert?

4. What do the different reactions to the knocking at the door show about Mr. and Mrs White?

7) The Industrial Revolution:

The Industrial revolution was a time of great change in British society in the late 1700's to the mid 1800's. During this time technology meant that less workers were needed on farms while more factories were built in the cities. The White's were among those few that could commute to a factory nearby but still live in a very isolated, out of the way, location. The accident that Herbert has, also raises a lot of questions about work place safety during that time.

Questions:

1. How might factory working conditions in the early 1900's have changed compared with conditions today?

2. How did the factory that Herbert worked at view its employees based on the visit from the Maw and Meggins representative?

In The Classroom

MOTIFS:

Groups of three:

The story is centred around patterns of three.

- The monkey's paw offers three wishes to three separate people.

- Three people in the White family.

- Mr. White is the third owner of the paw.

- Three visitors to the house.

- The Maw and Meggins representative walks past the house gate three times.

- Mrs White hears the third visitor on the third knock.

There are a number of associations of threes in Western culture. Christianity is based on the Holy Trinity, the Father, the Son and the Holy Spirit. Superstition dictates that to disregard the power of three is to disregard the Holy Trinity. As the saying goes "bad luck comes in threes". Perhaps the monkey's paw itself could be seen as having faith in a talisman (object) and viewed as disrespecting Christianity. In literature, threes are considered unnatural because by nature we have pairs (legs, eyes, hands, feet etc.)

SYMBOLS:

The Monkey's Paw:

The monkey's paw symbolises greed and desire and a willingness to place faith in something unnatural to satisfy them. The paw has a power to attract and seduce the White family. Mr. White rescues it from the flames even though he is uncertain of what he would wish for. The paw demonstrates its power by granting Mr. White's wish then killing Herbert in consequence before finally raising him from the grave. Even though the paw symbolises the power of greed and desire, ironically it may possess no power at all and Herbert's death may have been a coincidence as suspected by Mr. White and the knock on the door may have been a living visitor.

Chess:

Chess is often seen as a metaphor for life. The way it is played symbolises the choices in life, risk and daring may be accompanied by reward or death. Mr. White and Herbert play chess as they wait for Sergeant Major Morris and Mr. White loses due to a deadly mistake concerning his king. This is paralleled in the story also as mistakes in the story bear deadly consequences.

In The Classroom

LITERARY REFERENCES IN THE STORY:

The screenplay and the play both make reference to other books and stories. This is called "intertextuality", when one text makes reference to another. Sometimes the reference can be stated; however it can also be implied by similarities. The following are intertextual references in "the Monkey's Paw":

Aladdin and the Magic Lamp - "The Book of One thousand and One Nights- Arabian Nights."

Q. Why would Mrs White refer to Arabian Nights? What does it suggest about how she feels about the paw?

Faust- is a scholar in German legend who sells his soul in exchange for the devils service. It was popularised in a play called "The Tragical History of Doctor Faustus" by Christopher Marlow (c.1604).

Q. What moments can you think of in the story where Mr. White seems to be like Faust?

The Bible - the monkey's paw wriggling in Mr. White's hand like a snake is a reference to the biblical story of Adam and Eve, where greed causes them to betray God.

Q. Read Genesis 3:1-24 in the Bible "The Fall of Man". What do you think this has to do with "The Monkey's Paw"? What were the consequences for Adam and Eve's greed?

INTERESTINGLY:

Just as "The Monkey's Paw" makes intertextual references to other texts, there are lots of texts that make reference to "The Monkey's Paw". For example:

> Treehouse of Horror II - In the 1991 Halloween episode of The Simpsons, one of the stories is about how Homer gets a monkey's paw that grants him four wishes. Each member of the Simpson family (except for Marge) makes a wish, which have terrible consequences. In a humorous twist, Homer gladly gives the paw to his neighbor Ned Flanders, only for Ned's wishes to (apparently) go off without any of the usual consequences, causing Homer to grumble "I wish I had a monkey paw."

Q. Try and find other texts that refer to "The Monkey's Paw" in some way.

HORROR:

"The Monkey's Paw" is part of the horror genre. (A "genre" is a style or category of literature).

Literary historian J. A. Cuddon has defined the horror story as "a piece of fiction in prose of variable length... which shocks or even frightens the reader, or perhaps induces a feeling of repulsion or loathing." Cuddon, J.A. (1984). "Introduction". *The Penguin Book of Horror Stories*. Harmondsworth: Penguin. p. 11. ISBN 0-14-006799-X.

In The Classroom

Some of the elements in "The Monkey's Paw" that do this are:

- It is a Dark and Stormy Night.
- It is a Deserted Street. An isolated manor.
- Doors bang.
- Stairs creak.
- Ticking of the clock.
- Living with Death and Misery.

Q. Try and list any other elements or moments in "The Monkey's Paw" that adds to the atmosphere of being scary.

A MODERN PARABLE:

The word "parable" comes from the Greek word "parabola", meaning "comparison, illustration, analogy." A parable is a story that illustrates one or more instructive lessons or principles. "The Monkey's Paw" is referred to as a modern parable.

Q. What are the lessons that can be learned from "The Monkey's Paw"?

LESSON IDEAS:

Trial by Jury

It could be argued that Herbert's accidental death at the factory was the result of the actions of three of the players in "The Monkey's Paw". Is Sergeant Major Morris responsible for Herbert's death by giving the Monkey's Paw to the White's knowing it's power? Is Mr. White the guilty party because he actually made the wish? Or is Mrs White guilty of guiding Mr. White's hand like Lady Macbeth greedily urging him for more?

Make your classroom a courtroom where each character is put on trial for the death of Herbert White. Teams of students could build a case for (prosecution) or against (defence) the guilt of each of the three characters. The text must be used as evidence for actual events and motives. A student playing each character could be cross-examined by the prosecution and defence who would need to present a case before a jury and judge.

Profile Detective:

Choose a character from "The Monkey's Paw" and create a complete character profile of them. The profile could include:

- What they look like (physicality). Find evidence from the text.

- What do you think their age is? Why? Support your answer with evidence.

- What are their motivations in the story? Give evidence.

- Try to find clues in the text to tell you what their personality might be like.

Draw an illustration of what you think they would look like.

The Short Story:

Read the short story "The Monkey's Paw" by W.W Jacobs.
http://www.gutenberg.org/ebooks/12122.
The story was first written in 1906 as a short horror, moral tale.

- Compare the short story to the Screenplay, or Comic, or Play.

- Are there any differences? What are they? Explain why?

- What is more effective? What is less effective?

Radio-Play:

Re-write "The Monkey's Paw" as a radio-play in small groups and record it. You could also include some "foley" sound effects in the play.

Storyboard:

Choose one scene from "The Monkey's Paw" and create a storyboard for the scene.

Poster:

Design a poster for "The Monkey's Paw", including a catchy logline.

SPECIAL THANKS

Special thanks to A. Kelly, the extraordinary artist responsible for bringing the graphic novel into fruition. Thanks to Redtube and Bnpublishing for sorting out the less interesting aspects such as barcodes and ISBN numbers. Thank you to Indiwriter for bringing the book cover to life and to April Sadowski for taking on the daunting task of interior design. Picture of Shane Emmett is provided courtesy of H.Bartholomew. Above all, special thanks to the most beautiful editor on the planet, Josephine Gleeson.

CPSIA information can be obtained
at www.ICGtesting.com
Printed in the USA
LVOW04s2134221116
514152LV00007B/28/P

9 781632 270405